We dedicate this guide to all the women who embraced our original book, *Moon Mother, Moon Daughter ~ Myths and Rituals that Celebrate a Girl's Coming-of-Age*, and have created communities that have transformed the way we honor and celebrate our daughters, ourselves, and women everywhere.

Table of Contents

Moon Mother, Moon Daughter

MOON CIRCLES FACILITATOR'S GUIDE

Moon Mother, Moon Daughter

MOON CIRCLES FACILITATOR'S GUIDE

Janet Lucy and Terri Allison

co-authors of *Moon Mother, Moon Daughter*

Myths and Rituals that Celebrate a Girl's Coming-of-Age

SEVEN SEAS
PRESS

Santa Barbara, California

Library of Congress Cataloging-in-Publication data available

ISBN #978-1-940654-09-6

SEVEN SEAS
PRESS

Cover illustration © Helen D'Souza/www.helendsouza.com

Design by Isaac Hernández de Lipa/www.isaachernandez.com

Introduction

Thank you for choosing our book, *Moon Mother, Moon Daughter ~ Myths and Rituals that Celebrate a Girl's Coming-of-Age.* Approaching the coming-of-age years can be a time of anticipation, confusion, and curiosity for mothers, daughters and other coming-of-agers. It is our hope that sharing this book with your daughter alone, in small groups with others, or with more mothers and daughters will offer opportunities to grow together, create shared experiences, support each other, and build a foundation for conversations to come.

When *Moon Mother, Moon Daughter* was first published in 2002, many of these concepts—myths, rituals, goddess worship, even the moon—were still a little "out there" for mainstream culture. Since then, women all over the world have been using *Moon Mother, Moon Daughter* as a guide. We're delighted that the first and second editions have had such a wide reception, and are deeply appreciative of all the women who have reached out to us to affirm our vision. We've also been inspired by the requests we've received for additional resources, particularly a companion guide for facilitating groups. This new *Moon Mother, Moon Daughter ~ Moon Circles Facilitator's Guide* is our wholehearted response and is intended to be used alongside the book.

For the original book, we chose goddess myths and stories from around the world to represent the unique and diverse world cultures. We also

"From what I have heard and observed many women yearn to belong to a women's circle... for patriarchy to change, there has to be a millionth circle."

~ Jean Shinoda Bolen, M.D., from *The Millionth Circle—How to Change Ourselves and the World*

included themes and topics to illuminate our universal divine feminine qualities and values drawn from an ancient wisdom that are essential for all of us to remember. This new *Moon Circles Facilitator's Guide* is intended to be an even more expansive and inclusive version of the original book. We've added new voices and language to be more inclusive and reflective of our diverse humanity. *Moon Mother, Moon Daughter* is a celebration of the divine feminine spirit!

All-Inclusive Guide

Since *Moon Mother, Moon Daughter* was first published, awareness about gender identity has evolved and changed. We would like to emphasize that throughout this guide, and retrospectively throughout the original book, the terms "girls" and "women" are inclusive of *all female spirited* people—those who are women-identified, and people of marginalized genders. While *Moon Mother, Moon Daughter* is intended as a book for mothers and daughters, we understand that some people do not identify with the gender assigned at birth. In order to ensure that your group is inclusive of all, you may want to ask the participants what pronouns they prefer and adjust the use of gender-related terms to better reflect the composition of your group. You'll find we also use the term "participant" to refer to the "coming-of-agers" and parents in your group. Every moon circle will have its own unique membership!

In Chapter 10, "Moon Circle ~ Weaving the Web of Community," we have added a new section called "Expanding Our Community" that includes "The Way of Two-Spirit People," which honors two-spirit people as recognized in ancient and many modern Native American cultures. When we speak of or have transgender or nonbinary participants in our moon circles, it's important that we use respectful terminology and language. Please refer to the "Appendix for Gender-Inclusive Appropriate Language" at the end of this guide. We hope that this addition and Appendix will support you as you strengthen the web of an inclusive community.

Mothers

There are many different kinds of mothers. "Mother" is defined as a nurturing adult in one's life, and can include grandmothers, stepmothers, aunts, and mentors. Families with two dads can opt to send one dad (ideally it is the same parent every time) or choose a special woman in their daughter's life. This guide is inclusive of all kinds of families. If you are facilitating a group with girls only, keep in mind that a girl may not have a mother who is actively present in her life. Be mindful of this during sessions. If you are unsure how to proceed, you can check in with the girl herself—she may already have ideas, thoughts, and feelings about what will best support her.

Each chapter offers many opportunities to talk about similarities and differences. The chapters titled "Moon Reflection," "Moon Time," and "Moon Love" are ideally suited to explore this further, and each chapter will include some notes for your consideration.

Ages And Stages

Although maturity levels and readiness will vary, this book and guide can be used with a wide range of ages. It is important to be aware of the developmental stage that the girls are experiencing. We have found ages eight to thirteen are the most receptive and ready for the activities and exercises in the book. The topics and activities can be adapted for additional ages as well. For example, you might choose or adjust the writing prompts in the "Journal Activity" according to age groups. Some participants may be older or have already had some of these experiences (i.e., their first period) and they may enjoy these rituals retroactively.

Our vision is that these "Moon Circles" continue to ripple out far and wide, including and connecting us all together. After all, we all live under the same moon.

With love,

Janet and Terri

Getting Started!

Here are some simple guidelines we trust will help you facilitate your Moon Circle:

- Begin by deciding what kind of moon circle you want to offer. For example, coming-of-agers with one facilitator, or a parent-child group. We have offered both group formats. They each work equally well with their own set of pros and cons. Sometimes, coming-of-agers feel more at ease in a group of their peers. On the other hand, a mother-daughter/parent-child group can strengthen the bond between girls and their mothers and can create a shared language for them as they navigate adolescence.

- Set up a clear schedule for your meetings: weekly, monthly, or every two weeks; consistent time; two to three hours recommended. Sunday afternoons often work well.

- Give clear instructions: time frame, punctuality, and what to bring. Reminder emails or texts a couple of days before each group will lessen missed sessions and can help participants remember to bring their journals and anything else they might need.

- Set a predictable order of activities for each session. There is a suggested format in each chapter guide. Although specifics of activities will vary, a consistent and predictable order allows for comfort zones to be established and stretched.

- In the beginning, set an agenda with time frames for each activity. You can actually have it coincide with the real time (for example, "Read and discuss the myth from 2:00–2:30" as an entry in your agenda) to keep you on schedule.

- Read the corresponding chapter in the book as well as the guide for the chapter.

- Familiarize yourself with the "Group Format."

- Consider "Questions for Yourself" and notice what comes up for you around the topics and themes, which may influence or affect your participation in the group. We're all learning, discovering, and growing!

- Create the space with consideration for comfort and privacy. Your meeting place must be sacred, meaning free from entry/interruptions from anyone other than participants. Have a basket to hold all cell phones during the group.

- For each activity, gather the necessary art materials and have them ready for the meeting. Consider creating an art supply bin that contains basic art materials: Beads, buttons, baubles, fabric scraps, colored paper, glue, markers, paints, popsicle sticks, cotton balls, feathers, stones. This will provide a foundation for each activity.

- Be prepared with extra pens/pencils and paper. It's always good to have a box of Kleenex handy.

- Learn to be comfortable with pauses and silence. Sometimes there is knowing and understanding in the "in-between" spaces.

- In all mother-daughter groups, moms and girls alike participate in discussions and activities.

CONFIDENTIALITY

One of the most essential ways we create safety and trust in our moon circles is with the knowing and agreement that all of our shared experiences, stories, and writing are held sacred and kept confidential. That means the participants agree not to tell each other's stories or experiences outside of the circle. This is an understanding and agreement that must be made at your first meeting. It's also wise to occasionally remind everyone of this agreement.

These are the three most Frequently Asked Questions...
We'd love to hear if you have others!

1. HOW DO I HANDLE A CHRONICALLY LATE PARTICIPANT?

Find a time when you can be alone and speak non-judgmentally about some strategies for being on time. Ask how you can help. Even if participants continue to be late, start on time and warmly welcome them when they arrive.

2. HOW DO I MODERATE OVER-TALKERS AND QUIETER PARTICIPANTS?

Until you have established trust and a group culture, going around the circle in order, timing responses so that everyone has an equal amount of time, or inviting the "quiet" participants to share first are good strategies. Keep in mind that not all participants will want or need to talk as often as others. Trust that they are learning and growing in their own way.

3. CAN I CHARGE A FEE? IF SO, HOW MUCH? (GROUP FEE? MATERIALS FEE?)

This is entirely up to you. It is best to start with an anticipated budget. How many participants will there be? What will be the cost of materials, snacks, and other supplies? You can also charge for your time! Remember: Most families pay for summer camps, after school activities, and more, so this will not be an unexpected request. Some "Moon Circles" work as co-ops—sharing costs and taking turns preparing activities.

WHAT YOU'LL FIND IN THIS GUIDE

Chapters 1 through 11 will include these essential parts and then follow a consistent group format. We've included a recommended amount of time for each activity, which of course may vary from one meeting and chapter to another. We recommend using your last meeting (Chapter 12, "Moon Dance ~ Celebrating Coming-of-Age") for a celebration. Suggestions and details are listed there. Once the group is started and established, as the facilitator, take a look ahead at Chapter 12. By now, you will probably have a sense of what kind of celebratory ritual will work for your group. You can begin to talk about the idea of a celebration and have the girls start to think about what they might like to include. Allow for planning time during the Chapter 11 session.

1. PRE-GROUP CONSIDERATION FOR FACILITATORS AND QUESTIONS FOR YOURSELF

Allow yourself some time (at least 30 minutes) a few days before the meeting to consider the questions for yourself. Journaling may be helpful. You might also like to discuss them with another mom or female friend. We're all learning and exploring these concepts together, many for the first time. Be kind with yourself and offer gentle reminders to the group as well.

At the beginning of each chapter you will find quotes we have chosen as additional inspiration for the chapter theme. You might like to take some time on your own or within the circle to reflect on the words.

2. A LIST OF THE CHAPTER'S MAIN THEMES (AND SOME STORIES TO LOOK FOR!)

We've picked out the themes we feel are most essential in each chapter as well as some stories about "real girls and women" that support them.

3. BEGIN / CHECK IN WITH A REFLECTIVE QUESTION (15 min.)

We recommend beginning each meeting with everyone sitting in a circle so all participants can see each other, and then asking a reflective question. A reflective question is designed to formally begin the session and is based on the theme. It invites each participant to bring her true self into the circle. A reflective question is open-ended and there is no right or wrong answer. Each participant has an opportunity to answer briefly taking just a minute or two. They should be allowed to "pass" if they are not ready to share. (This is true during any activity.) This is a time for centering. Each chapter guide will offer a reflective question as a suggestion, but feel free to adjust the questions to fit the group. As the facilitator, you can use this time to gauge where everyone is and adjust the session as needed. For example, during one session it was clear that the group needed to process something that had happened at school. We took time to talk about it and we were even able to make a connection to the myth and the theme of the day. If you choose to begin this way, be sure to follow the "circle discussion format" so each girl has an opportunity to be heard (and being heard is the most important thing). You might simply ask, "What did you experience today? How did you feel?" You will need to keep this extra conversation "time-bound" so you have time for other activities.

4. THE MYTHS (20 min.)

Read the myth featured in the chapter aloud. Ask: What did you hear in the myth? What did you notice as you listened to the story? What stood out for you? What are you curious about? As the facilitator, have some of your own ideas to offer if responses are slow, perhaps a partial reflection, i.e., "This myth reminds me of..." Or, consider the phrase, "I noticed..." then perhaps ask the girls this same question, "What did you notice?" "Noticing" is a power tool!

5. ART ACTIVITY (45 min.)

Before each meeting, choose one of the activities from your copy of *Moon Mother, Moon Daughter* and add any specific ingredients needed for the chosen activity. Feel free to adapt or modify the activity to use the resources you have on hand. You will find all of the instructions for the specific activities in the book. Use your imagination to fill in the gaps! Allow the girls to use their imaginations, too, with the materials you have. You can also use a cooperative format and have other mothers in the group bring the materials for the activity. Gentle reminder: Gather all the materials ahead of time.

6. JOURNAL ACTIVITY ~ WRITING AND WITNESSING (30 min.)

We've created *By the Light of the Moon ~ A Moon Mother, Moon Daughter Companion Journal* to use for the journal writing activities. You may want to purchase one for everyone in the group, or they may each purchase one or bring their own. Having journals that are specific to the group and similar in style can create a sense of a shared journey of writing and discovery. It's also a way to ensure that every person in the group has a journal. You can budget the cost of them as part of determining your fee or ask for reimbursement.

Each chapter guide will include several writing prompts based on the themes and myth. The participants will use their journals to write spontaneously from these prompts. You can offer all or just one or two. Keep the time short. Five minutes per prompt is recommended. After they have completed their journal writing, invite each participant to read aloud. Instruct the others to listen attentively with receptive body language, facing the speaker and without attending to other distractions. Then, reflect back with a simple sentence: "I liked when you wrote…" or "I loved that you wrote…" Most importantly, the listeners do not talk about themselves. They only "witness" and reflect the writer/reader. This may take them out of their comfort zones and will definitely take practice. Once they understand the process, it will be something they will use throughout the book and hopefully in their lives. In this guide, Chapter 4, "Moon Wind ~ Finding Your Voice," offers more listening and speaking practice.

A note about "closure": It's always important to center and close the circle after each session. The "Writing and Witnessing" time with all sitting in a circle will facilitate this and bring your session to a natural close. An excellent "closure" question at the end of each circle is simply, "What will you take with you today?" A one-word response is ideal!

7. FACILITATOR'S NOTES

At the end of each chapter, you'll find a place for your own reflections with prompts for journaling. This is an opportunity for you to reflect on the session, note what you experienced, and clarify what might be useful or beneficial for the next session. These notes are for you and will be helpful for the next meeting and/or if you facilitate a moon circle again. If possible, do this right away while your thoughts are fresh. Also, there are wide margins on each page for your notes as well.

8. FURTHER RESOURCES

Please note, this book is not intended to be a comprehensive guide for each concept in the chapters. There are many additional resources to support you so that participants have a factual understanding of their bodies and more complex issues if desired, or to guide you when difficult questions arise. We have included some additional resources at the end of this guide. There is an extensive Bibliography at the back of *Moon Mother, Moon Daughter*.

Here We Go! Getting Started And Centering With Chapter 1

Chapter 1 is ideal for a "practice session." You will have an opportunity to introduce basic concepts and practice group format. One thing we'd like to emphasize is the value of process. This group is designed to offer the girls a new way to imagine themselves, and it may be challenging for them to get away from how they have been conditioned to perform. Gentle reminders and guidance will help everyone to become more authentic as time goes on. Be gentle with yourself and the group as you navigate this journey.

1
Moon Wisdom
Living by the Moon

●○○●●

The Modern-Day Demeter and Persephone

The modern-day Demeter and Persephone have a close and loving relationship. They understand that their own relationship waxes and wanes and has its own natural seasons. Like all cycles of beginnings and endings, they know that their relationship comes full circle, and through it all they stay connected.

◑○○

PRE-GROUP CONSIDERATION FOR FACILITATORS AND QUESTIONS FOR YOURSELF

Chapter 1 is an invitation to explore the wisdom of the moon, the wheel of the year, holy days and holidays, rituals, celebrations, the seasons of a woman's life, and the changing nature of the mother-daughter relationship.

What do you notice about these cycles and seasons, holy days, and celebrations? How is a ritual similar to or different from a holiday tradition? Do you consciously create rituals in your life? What do you notice about your changing mother-daughter relationship?

A Note: The ideas and activities in each chapter are likely to be new. The novelty may be inspiring to some and intimidating to others. Behaviors

"A woman in harmony with her spirit is like a river flowing. She goes where she will without pretense and arrives at her destination, prepared to be herself and only herself."

~ Maya Angelou

may range from loud and silly to quiet and withdrawn. Just know this is all normal and it will take some practice for everyone to feel comfortable. Kindness, respect, and acceptance are the guiding principles!

CHAPTER THEMES

- Rituals and traditions / holidays and holy days
- Lunar cycles and moon phases; seasons and "The Wheel of the Year"
- The value of community and sustained mother-daughter connection; the changing mother-daughter relationship.

STORIES IN CHAPTER THAT HIGHLIGHT THEMES

Winter Solstice ritual.

The "vision-seeding ritual" in Chapter 1 is an easy, inspiring, and fun introduction to creating rituals. It can be included in your Chapter 1 meeting or saved and offered for Winter Solstice or a New Moon ritual.

CHECK-IN ~ REFLECTIVE QUESTION

Ask: How often do you notice the moon in the sky? Do you sometimes see her during the day? What do notice about her changing face?

Ask: What do you imagine when you think of a goddess? Are you familiar with any?

READ "The Myth of Demeter and Persephone"

Ask: What did you hear in the myth? What did you notice as you listened to the story? What stood out for you? What are you curious about? As the facilitator, have some of your own ideas to offer if responses are slow, perhaps a partial reflection, i.e., "This myth reminds me of…" Or consider the phrase, "I noticed…" then perhaps ask, "What did you notice?" "Noticing" is a power tool!

ART ACTIVITY

MOON PHASES

Create a visual of the eight phases of the moon. You will need: dark blue or black construction paper, pale yellow, white, or silver paper or cardboard. Glue sticks and scissors. Glitter for stars.

● New Moon

◐ Crescent Moon

◑ First Quarter Moon

◑ Gibbous Moon

○ Full Moon

◗ Disseminating Moon

◗ Last Quarter Moon

◗ Balsamic Moon

Identifying the phases in the sky: Encourage everyone to look for these different moon phases in the sky and match their "visual" with what they see. Some phases are visible at night, others in the daylight. Ask them what they notice and what time of day they see each phase.

For additional information and details about moon phases, rising and setting times, visit mooncircles.com.

JOURNAL ACTIVITY ~ WRITING AND WITNESSING

Prompts:

My idea of a goddess is...

I notice the moon when...

Looking at the night sky...

When the moon is full and bright...

My favorite season is...

Facilitator's Notes

This chapter I noticed…

Facilitating this session…

My favorite moment was…

Next time, I will…

Other thoughts:

2
Moon Light
Awakening Inner Wisdom and Intuition

●◗○◖●

The Modern-Day Tara

Today's Tara knows that her intuition is an essential source of guidance. She creates a spiritual practice that quiets her mind and allows her to listen to her inner voice. Like Vasalisa, she has been gifted by her mother with a strong sense of herself and her intuition. As she makes her way out into the world, she carries this gift with her.

◗○◖

"For there is always light,
if only we're brave enough
to see it
If only we're brave enough
to be it."

~ Amanda Gorman,
Youth Poet Laureate

PRE-GROUP CONSIDERATION FOR FACILITATORS AND QUESTIONS FOR YOURSELF

"Creating Spiritual Practices and Teaching Our Daughters to be Intuitive" are the essential invitations in this chapter. Spiritual practices create the quiet and stillness that allow the voice of intuition to be heard.

How do you experience your intuition? What are the practices that allow you to listen to the voice within?

A Note: Puberty is a stage when self-confidence begins to waver, often coinciding with the sudden changes in the body. Confident seven- or eight-year-olds may become reticent and self-doubting tweens. This is a time they may also become more approval seeking rather than true to themselves, especially in relationship to their peers. This is an ideal opportunity to reinforce the concept of authenticity versus approval, and note the difference between impulsivity and intuition. One of the most important things we can teach our daughters and continually reinforce is to trust their intuition and themselves.

CHAPTER THEMES

- Creating spiritual practices
- Teaching our daughters to be intuitive
- Listening to an inner voice
- Discovering intuitive body wisdom

STORIES IN CHAPTER THAT HIGHLIGHT THEMES

Hearing an inner voice in the silence and solitude after Melitta's death.

CHECK-IN ~ REFLECTIVE QUESTION

Ask: Have you heard of the term "intuition"? What does it mean to you? How do you experience it? A feeling? An inner voice? If you feel the group needs a little guidance, you could ask: Has there been a time when you "knew" something but couldn't quite put your finger on it and then later, when you checked in with a friend or your mom, you realized your intuition was right? (Facilitator could lead and model an example of this.)

This chapter contains two wonderful myths, "The Myth of Tara, the Tibetan Goddess of Inner Wisdom" and "The Doll in Her Pocket: Vasalisa the Wise." We suggest you focus on either "The Myth of Tara" and the Tara Candle-Making activity or "Vasalisa" and the Doll-Making activity.

READ "The Doll in Her Pocket: Vasalisa the Wise"

Ask: What did you hear in the myth? What did you notice as you listened to the story? What stood out for you? What are you curious about? As the facilitator, have some of your own ideas to offer if responses are slow, and offer a partial reflection, i.e., "This myth reminds me of…" Or consider the phrase, "I noticed…" then perhaps ask the girls with this same question, "What did you notice?" "Noticing" is a power tool!

ART ACTIVITY

INTUITION DOLLS

The Safety Sensor Activity and Doll-Making Activity can go hand in hand. Consider completing "The Safety Sensor Activity" before writing.

JOURNAL ACTIVITY ~ WRITING AND WITNESSING

There are many writing activities and prompts to choose from here. Pick one or two, then encourage everyone, including parents, to do some of the others in between sessions. They can write the extra prompts in their journals to use at home. Remind everyone that sometimes writing about a problem or question brings an intuitive answer.

SPIRITUAL PRACTICE/LISTENING FOR AN INNER VOICE ~
MAKE A LIST
(Collecting ideas for spiritual practices could also be a group activity.)

My ideas for a spiritual practice are:

1.

2.

3.

Prompts:

When I sit quietly...

Sometimes I get a feeling...

Listening for an inner voice...

Another way I find quiet is...

THE SAFETY SENSOR
(Guided instructions are in *Moon Mother, Moon Daughter*)

Prompts:

When I'm excited my body feels...

When I'm scared my body feels...

When I'm calm my body feels...

Facilitator's Notes

This chapter I noticed...

Facilitating this session...

My favorite moment was...

Next time, I will...

Other thoughts:

3
Moon Shadow
Spending Time Alone

●◐○○●

The Modern-Day Artemis

The Artemis of today is as comfortable in nature as she is in cyber-space. She is aware of her own natural rhythm and seeks to balance her active and busy life with healthy doses of downtime. She knows that creating time to rest and restore her energy is essential to her well-being, and that spending quiet time alone replenishes her inner world and nourishes her soul. She has an independent spirit and radiates a strong sense of self.

◐○●

"When change comes, you gotta slow down and take note of it. In the midst of that change is all the possibility in the world."

~ Dr. Bertice Berry

PRE-GROUP CONSIDERATION FOR FACILITATORS AND QUESTIONS FOR YOURSELF

Chapter 3 is an invitation to explore spending time alone.

How do you feel about spending time alone? What does "sacred space" mean to you? How do you experience "being" versus "doing"? What is your favorite way to connect with nature?

A Note: With social media, after school activities and our "togetherness" culture, it is rare that anyone this age chooses or has much time to spend alone or without a device to keep them company. Go slowly—at first, they may need to imagine what it would be like if they were alone. This is a time when you can encourage mothers to allow (and maybe even schedule!) time for their daughters to spend time alone.

CHAPTER THEMES

- Spending time alone; creating conscious solitude
- The essential value of downtime and rest
- Sacred space
- Artemis and nature
- Natural rhythms; ebbs and flows; being and doing

STORIES IN CHAPTER THAT HIGHLIGHT THEMES

Jordan's "vision quest"; sleeping outside.

CHECK-IN ~ REFLECTIVE QUESTION

In this session we are going to talk about spending time alone. It is important to distinguish that spending time alone is different than being isolated or lonely.

Ask: What is the difference to you? Have you spent time alone without being lonely?

READ "The Myth of Artemis"

Ask: What did you hear in the myth? What did you notice as you listened to the story? What stood out for you? What are you curious about? As the facilitator, have some of your own ideas to offer if responses are slow and offer a partial reflection, i.e., "This myth reminds me of..." Or consider the phrase, "I noticed..." then perhaps ask, "What did you notice?" "Noticing" is a power tool!

OUTDOOR ACTIVITY ~ "BACK TO NATURE"

Create an outdoor activity with your group. This could be just a couple hours, like a hike, or an overnight camping trip. (This might be how you meet for Chapter 4 or a bonus activity!) You could also create an easy backyard sleepover, choosing a special night to sleep outside. Include a quiet journaling time like Jordan experienced during her "Vision Quest." Invite the participants to write about what they see, smell, hear... including their inner voice. Sketchbooks are fun, too! Pressed flowers and leaves? Stargazing? A meteor shower? Full moon rise? (Check your almanac!)

ART ACTIVITY

PERSONAL ALTARS

Gather materials to make personal altars. An empty shoebox (standing upright or horizontally) could set the stage. The girls can decorate their altars with paint, fabric, paper, and glue. Later, each girl can include her own personal symbols (i.e., stones, feathers, shells, dolls, photos) that add meaning to her altar when she gets home. Suggest adding symbols of what she loves, values, or wishes.

PRE-WRITING ACTIVITY ~ SPENDING TIME ALONE

"IDENTIFYING SOLO-TIME ACTIVITIES"

Invite your group to share or to make a list of activities they enjoy doing alone, or might like to experience alone. Suggest several categories, i.e., active (dancing to music), creative (an art project), stillness (reading an enjoyable book). You might also facilitate a brief discussion: "What is the value/purpose of quiet alone time?" "How does the idea feel to you?" "Could it be a gift?" (You might like to refer to Jordan's experience.)

JOURNAL ACTIVITY ~ WRITING AND WITNESSING

Prompts:

Spending time alone feels…

A solo activity I love…

Or, a solo activity I would like to try…

When I'm in nature…

My altar reflects…

Some symbols I'll add…

Facilitator's Notes

This chapter I noticed...

Facilitating this session...

My favorite moment was...

Next time, I will...

Other thoughts:

4
Moon Wind
Finding Your Voice

●◐○○● ●

The Modern-Day Oya

The modern-day Oya speaks clearly and confidently from her heart. She acknowledges her true feelings and expresses them authentically. She knows her personal rights and expresses herself assertively. She values being listened to and listening to others. Her relationships with others are kind, honest, and respectful.

◐○◐

PRE-GROUP CONSIDERATION FOR FACILITATORS AND QUESTIONS FOR YOURSELF

Chapter 4 focuses on strengthening one's voice and becoming a thoughtful listener.

How do you experience yourself as a listener? How do you feel about speaking in front of small or large groups? What gives you confidence? What do you fear?

A Note: This is a good time to reinforce the conversation about confidence from Chapter 2. This too can be an age where girls lose their voices. What does it mean to speak up, for oneself, one's values, or in support of each other? What does it mean to stand in solidarity? Assertive girls are often seen as "bossy," as opposed to their male peers who when displaying the

"Practice developing your 'yes' and your 'no' so you are clear what is true for you. Notice when your head is blocking your heart or you are over-thinking your 'yes.' How is that different from when you are feeling your 'yes' deep inside you?"

~ Dr. Tererai Trent,
The Awakened Woman

same behavior are more likely to be labeled "leaders." Talk explicitly about this difference—have they noticed it themselves? What ideas do they have about changing these narratives?

CHAPTER THEMES

- Listening to our daughters
- Daughters finding their voices

STORIES IN CHAPTER THAT HIGHLIGHT THEMES

Austin's shyness and the special stone; Mikaila's question about her soccer game.

CHECK-IN ~ REFLECTIVE QUESTION

Ask: Do you prefer to talk or listen?

Make sure that participants keep their answers brief, then follow with a short group discussion about the characteristics of "good listeners" (more on "Compassionate Listening" in Chapter 11) and "respectful talkers."

READ "The Myth of Oya"

Ask: What did you hear in the myth? What did you notice as you listened to the story? What stood out for you? What are you curious about? As the facilitator, have some of your own ideas to offer if responses are slow and offer a partial reflection, i.e., "This myth reminds me of…" Or consider the phrase, "I noticed…" then ask, "What did you notice?" "Noticing" is a power tool!

As Facilitator, you might consider these concepts: "Power of words," "confident communication," and "nonverbal body language." You can ask the girls what they believe these concepts mean, or explain.

SPEAKING AND LISTENING

For the next activity, you might like to practice the "Talking Stick" or "Council Circle" activities with your group, as described in the book.

LISTENING PRACTICE ACTIVITY

Put these statements on strips of paper in a basket:

Tell about a time you were…

Scared

Surprised

Mad

Sad

Laughing

Homesick

Felt loved

Tell the group the purpose of this speaking and listening activity is to practice listening from the heart. Remind them they are listening to hear, see, and understand, rather than listening to respond. Building empathetic listening skills takes practice and intentionality.

Invite each participant to take a turn picking one and sharing their story in three to five minutes. (You can divide the time depending on how many are in the group.)

Ask the others to listen with receptive body language, facing the speaker and making eye contact. After each story is shared, ask them, "What did you hear?" Instruct them to keep their responses brief. Remind them it is not their job to fix, interpret, or dismiss what they have heard. (For example, "It's not that bad," or "It will get better," or "That's not true, I think you're pretty," or even, "The same thing happened to me.") Instead, comments like, "Wow! That must have been scary/sad/exciting," focuses on the speaker's experience and builds understanding and trust.

"There's power in allowing yourself to be known and heard, in owning your unique story, in using your authentic voice. And there's grace in being willing to know and hear others."

~ Michelle Obama

ART ACTIVITY

EMOTIONAL TOUCHSTONES

If you don't have access to stones, you can use cardboard or construction paper to cut out "stones." (Other materials can also be substituted for stones, i.e., wooden blocks, sea glass... be creative and resourceful!)

TALKING STICK

Provide or have the girls bring a stick or dowel to create their own talking stick. These can be decorated with ribbon, yarn, string, beads and feathers, anything that makes them feel fun and inspiring to use.

JOURNAL ACTIVITY ~ WRITING AND WITNESSING

Prompts:

When I speak in front of my class...

Talking to adults...

Talking to other kids...

When I listen to others...

Facilitator's Notes

This chapter I noticed…

Facilitating this session…

My favorite moment was…

Next time, I will…

Other thoughts:

5
Moon Dreams
Exploring Your Dreams

●◖○○◗●

The Modern-Day Dreaming Goddess

The modern-day dreaming goddess is valued for her ability to dream. She invites her dreams to guide and inspire her. She recognizes that her dreams support her intuition, creativity, and aspirations. She welcomes the dream goddess through her prayers and meditations each night as she drifts off to sleep. She dares to dream and knows that what she can see, she can be. She knows that both her nighttime and daytime dreams can reveal the path to her highest potential. She knows her dreams connect her to other women and are a bridge to her ancestors.

◖○○

PRE-GROUP CONSIDERATION FOR FACILITATORS AND QUESTIONS FOR YOURSELF

There are many types of dreams. In this chapter we discuss three: Nighttime dreams, daydreams, and dreams as aspirations and wishes.

Do you remember your dreams? What do you notice about the themes and images in your dreams?

A Note: This might be a stage when the participants in your group have trouble sleeping. Hormonal changes, moon rhythms, electronic devices, and nightmares can interfere with quality sleep. This is a good time to

"If all the woman of the world
recorded their dreams for a
single week
and laid them all end to end,
we would recover
the last million years
of women's hymns and chants
and dances,
all of women's art and stories,
and medicines,
all of women's lost histories."

~ Dr. Clarissa Pinkola Estés

reinforce healthy sleep habits and beneficial bedtime routines and rituals. Research is showing that lack of quality sleep is a major issue and contributes to the overall stress, health and mental health challenges that are prevalent today.

CHAPTER THEMES

- Remembering your dreams
- Keeping a dream journal
- Our daughters as dreamers
- Dreams as wishes and aspirations

STORIES IN CHAPTER THAT HIGHLIGHT THEMES

Nona's offerings; Sarah, the dreamer.

CHECK-IN ~ REFLECTIVE QUESTION

There are many kinds of dreams. Nighttime dreams, daydreams and dreams that are hopes or wishes.

Ask: What kinds of dreams do you have? What kinds of dreams do you remember?

READ "The Myth of the Dreaming Goddess"

Ask: What did you hear in the myth? What did you notice as you listened to the story? What stood out for you? What are you curious about? As the facilitator, have some of your own ideas to offer if responses are slow and offer a partial reflection, i.e., "This myth reminds me of..." Or consider the phrase, "I noticed..." then perhaps ask, "What did you notice?" "Noticing" is a power tool!

ART ACTIVITY

DREAM PILLOWS

There are many imaginative and inspiring ideas for exploring and expressing dreams in THE ART OF DREAMING ~ ACTIVITIES FOR CREATIVE PLAY. These can also be incorporated into a sleepover.

JOURNAL ACTIVITY ~ WRITING AND WITNESSING

There are many to choose from. Pick one or two then encourage everyone including parents to do some of the others in-between sessions. You may want to print some of these to take home, share, and/or practice alone or with each other.

"DEAR DREAM GODDESS" ~ WRITE A DREAM PRAYER OR LETTER TO THE DREAM GODDESS

When introducing this activity, invite the girls to consider the following possibilities:

What would you like to ask her? Have you had a recurring scary dream you'd like her to help you change? Write an intention for your dream life. Ask her to bring the resolution to a problem; a fresh idea, story, poem, or song; or courage to face a challenge. Keep your journal next to your bed to read each night and to jot down any dreams you remember when you wake up. When you make this a regular practice, you will be empowered to use your dreams as a resource for the rest of your life.

Prompts:

Remembering my dreams…

Guided by my dreams…

Following my dreams…

Prompts from the Myth:

Imagining the dream caves…

Sleeping and dreaming…

Awakening with a message…

Dreams as Wishes and Aspirations ~ Dreaming of extraordinary or magical powers is natural. What magical power do you wish you had? What is your "super power" or what would you like it to be? How might a "super power" help you in your life? Write about it!

Facilitator's Notes

This chapter I noticed…

Facilitating this session…

My favorite moment was…

Next time, I will…

Other thoughts:

6

Moon Beam

Expressing Your Creativity

●○○○●

The Modern-Day Hina

Today's Hina is free to embrace her creative spirit. Inspired by her own inner muses, she explores different ways to express her creative passions and likes to spend quiet moments with her imagination. She knows that her creativity is the vital life-force energy that is connected to her spirit. She confidently reveals her creative gifts and celebrates the unique expression of her soul.

◑○○

PRE-GROUP CONSIDERATION FOR FACILITATORS AND QUESTIONS FOR YOURSELF

Art impacts our lives in many ways beyond crafts and creative projects. This chapter invites us to savor the creative process and look for inspiration everywhere.

What is a muse? What inspires or ignites your creative spirit? How do you express your creative spirit? Consider the difference between the words "passion" and "curiosity." For many, curiosity is easier to follow while the awareness of one's passion may not be clear.

Michelle Obama reminds us that art is reflective of cultures and traditions as the "Myth of Hina" illustrates.

"Creativity is an energy. It's a precious energy, and it's something to be protected. A lot of people take for granted that they're a creative person, but I know from experience, feeling it in myself, it is a magic; it is an energy. And it can't be taken for granted."

~ Ava DuVernay

"The arts are not just a nice thing to have or to do if there is free time or if one can afford it. Rather, paintings and poetry, music and fashion, design and dialogue, they all define who we are as a people and provide an account of our history for the next generation."

As you prepare, remember that art impacts our lives in many ways beyond crafts and creative projects. Michelle Obama reminds us that art is reflective of cultures and traditions as the "Myth of Hina" illustrates.

A Note: Because we live in a competitive culture, the girls may be tempted to compare their creations. Talk about it beforehand and then gently remind them throughout the session that all our creations are unique and valuable, just like they are. You might even want to encourage them to try "not comparing" in their classes at school and sharing this idea/awareness with classmates.

CHAPTER THEMES

- Exploring and expressing creativity in many forms (Music! Dance!)
- Creativity is messy
- Creative adventures

STORIES IN CHAPTER THAT HIGHLIGHT THEMES

Austin's and Emma's creative expression.

CHECK-IN ~ REFLECTIVE QUESTION

A muse is someone or something that inspires or sparks our creativity, like the night sky and moon, music, and other forms of beauty. It might also be an idea or a curiosity.

Ask: Do you have a muse? How do you follow your curiosity?

READ "The Myth of Hina, Polynesian Moon Goddess" or "Calling the Muse: The Nine Muses—Greek Goddesses of Creativity and Inspiration"

Ask: What did you hear in the myth? What did you notice as you listened to the story? What stood out for you? What are you curious about? As the facilitator, have some of your own ideas to offer if responses are slow and offer a partial reflection, i.e., "This myth reminds me of..." Or consider the phrase, "I noticed..." then perhaps ask, "What did you notice?" "Noticing" is a power tool!

ART ACTIVITY

PAINTING TAPA MUDCLOTH

MAKING TREASURE-FILLED CANDLES

(Another option is to buy clear glass luminarias and collage them with chosen images.)

JOURNAL ACTIVITY ~ WRITING AND WITNESSING

Prompts:

Being creative…

I'm curious about…

My favorite muse…

An idea I have is…

Facilitator's Notes

This chapter I noticed...

Facilitating this session...

My favorite moment was...

Next time, I will...

Other thoughts:

7

Moon Reflection
Honoring Your Body

●◗○◖●

The Modern-Day Gaia

The modern-day Gaia accepts the uniqueness of her own earth body and revels in its power. Through adornment and self-loving care, she honors and celebrates the sacredness of her body. Today's Gaia knows that true beauty comes from within. From her radiant core she lets her light shine.

◗○◖

"You all can judge my body all you want, but at the end of the day it's MY body. I love it and I'm comfortable in my own skin."

~ Simone Biles via Twitter

PRE-GROUP CONSIDERATION FOR FACILITATORS AND QUESTIONS FOR YOURSELF

In our culture, there is a glorified ideal body type, making it difficult for differing women, girls, and gender nonconforming people to love and accept their natural bodies.

How do you feel about your body type, size, shape, and weight? Do you discuss dieting, being too fat or too thin, or how much you weigh at home? How do you love and care for your body?

A Note: People are aware of the constant emphasis on body and body image. Coming-of-agers' bodies are, or soon will be, changing rapidly. This is a good time to talk about those natural changes, as well as about social media and its influence on self-esteem. Your time together can help them devise their own strategies for challenging the negative personal and societal beliefs about their bodies. As important adults in their lives, one of our essential roles is to model self-love and self-acceptance. Equally important is for each and every person to know their body is their own, as emphasized in the following quote:

> "Children's bodies are not public property. Teaching children bodily autonomy, privacy, and consent are the cornerstones of raising radical self-love humans."
> ~ Sonya Renee Taylor, The Body is Not an Apology

CHAPTER THEMES

- Body image and acceptance
- Correlation between the earth and the female body
- Inner beauty versus outer beauty; body beautification and adornment

STORIES IN CHAPTER THAT HIGHLIGHT THEMES

Sarah's question about fat and being thinner; Austin's and Sarah's different body types; Mikaila's and her friends' varying shapes and sizes; Sarah's body art.

CHECK-IN ~ REFLECTIVE QUESTION

Ask: What is something amazing about your body?

READ "The Myth of Gaia"

Ask: What did you hear in the myth? What did you notice as you listened to the story? What stood out for you? What are you curious about? As the facilitator, have some of your own ideas to offer if responses are slow and offer a partial reflection, i.e., "This myth reminds me of…" Or consider the phrase, "I noticed…" then perhaps ask, "What did you notice?" "Noticing" is a power tool!!

ART ACTIVITY

GODDESS ART AND BODY TALK

BODY SCULPT

If you'd like, combine the two activities shown in Chapter 7 sidebars by sharing pictures from a "goddess art" book before offering clay, modeling clay, or beeswax for sculpting.

JOURNAL ACTIVITY ~ WRITING AND WITNESSING

Use the "Guided Visualization of Inner Beauty" as an empowering meditation. You can add to the meditation in the chapter; for example, "See yourself standing tall."

Prompts:

Relaxing my body…
Feeling the warmth of the sun…
Standing tall…
My amazing body…
Like the earth…

For older girls:

When I look at photos on social media (i.e., Instagram), I notice…

Write a poem. You might also like to consider this poem as inspiration for the journal activity. Read the poem aloud. You can offer the girls the prompt, "My body is…" and invite them to write their own poem.

THIS BODY II ~ RENÉE WATSON
My body is
perfect and
imperfect and
Black and
girl and
big and
thick hair and
short legs and
scraped knee and
healed scar and
heart beating and
hands that hold and
voice that bellows and
feet that dance and
arms that embrace and
my momma's eyes and
my daddy's smile and
my grandma's hope and
my body is masterpiece and
my body is mine.

"You can't eat beauty, it doesn't feed you… beauty was not a thing that I could acquire or consume, it was something that I just had to be. You can't rely on how you look to sustain you. What actually sustains us, what is fundamentally beautiful, is compassion—for yourself and for those around you. That kind of beauty inflames the heart and enchants the soul."

~ Lupita Nyong'o

Facilitator's Notes

This chapter I noticed…

Facilitating this session…

My favorite moment was…

Next time, I will…

Other thoughts:

8
Moon Time
Celebrating Menstruation

●◐○◑●

The Modern-Day Hera

Today's Hera understands the correlation between the monthly cycles of the moon and her own "moon cycles." She honors and appreciates each phase of her own moon time and the changing opportunities offered throughout each cycle. She knows that menarche is a powerful passage to a new stage of her life. She welcomes her first moon with celebration.

◐○◑

"Study after study shows that women in most cultures are socialized to question their voices and distrust their bodies."

~ Dr. Tererai Trent,
The Awakened Woman

PRE-GROUP CONSIDERATION FOR FACILITATORS AND QUESTIONS FOR YOURSELF

Chapter 8 introduces new perspectives about menstruation and First Moon experiences.

What do you remember about your first moon? (Refer to the "Just for Mothers" sidebar in Chapter 8 of the book) How would your life have been different if there had been a Women's Lodge or if you had experienced a ritual like in the "Myth of Hera"? What do you appreciate about your menstrual cycle? Do you see it as a blessing or "the curse"? If your personal first moon experience was traumatic, this chapter may be an opportunity to revisit and rewrite your story.

A Note: The group might feel shy or uncomfortable talking about menstruation. Cultural norms often prevent or inhibit us from speaking about menstruation. Some may be unfamiliar with it or have only had information from school health classes, friends, or media. The reflective question below will help you gauge what knowledge they have and what is missing. You may want to prepare to share some basic information. This chapter theme celebrates menstruation, but no need to push that spirit if it doesn't feel like something to celebrate yet! The girls will come to their own understanding (and hopefully, appreciation!) in their own time. The most important thing is to model a positive perspective.

Some girls may already be menstruating and some members of the group may not menstruate at all. Not every female spirited person or woman has a vulva or uterus. Activities and discussion can be adjusted to meet the needs of the participants. If a participant has had a negative first experience, this chapter may also be an opportunity for healing

CHAPTER THEMES

- Celebrating menarche ~ first moon (other cultures and our modern girls)
- Valuing and honoring the menstrual cycle
- Correlating our menstrual cycles with the moon phases, particularly the New and Full Moons

STORIES IN CHAPTER THAT HIGHLIGHT THEMES

Mikaila's, Austin's, and Angelika's First Moon celebrations.

CHECK-IN ~ REFLECTIVE QUESTION

Ask: What have you learned about menstruation? How do you feel about it?

READ "The Myth of Hera, Goddess of the New Moon"

Ask: What did you hear in the myth? What did you notice as you listened to the story? What stood out for you? What are you curious about? As the facilitator, have some of your own ideas to offer if responses are slow and offer a partial reflection, i.e., "This myth reminds me of…" Or consider the phrase, "I noticed…" then perhaps ask, "What did you notice?" "Noticing" is a power tool!

ART ACTIVITY

FIRST MOON KIT

For moms and girls who have already started their periods, they can create a "Moon Time Kit" for their next period. If menstruation isn't relevant for any participants, consider suggesting a "Self-Care Kit" with nourishment for body love and pampering.

Chapter 8 is filled with ideas for creating first moon rituals that you can discuss with the participants and their parents.

JOURNAL ACTIVITY ~ WRITING AND WITNESSING

Choose the any of the prompts that pertain to your group:

For my first moon…

For my next moon… (For girls who are menstruating)

When I have my first period…

When I started my first period…

When I think about / talk about menstruation…

Facilitator's Notes

This chapter I noticed...

Facilitating this session...

My favorite moment was...

Next time, I will...

Other thoughts:

9
Moon Love
Discovering Sexuality

●◐○◑●

The Modern-Day Aphrodite

The modern-day Aphrodite is a "virgin goddess," meaning that she is true to her deepest self. She makes conscious choices that honor her body, heart, and soul. She knows that true intimacy comes with an open, honest, and close relationship with someone she can trust. She values intimate friendships and relationships and understands the difference between intimacy and sexuality. She is empowered with knowledge about her body and about sex. She knows that her sexuality is sacred.

◐○◑

PRE-GROUP CONSIDERATION FOR FACILITATORS AND QUESTIONS FOR YOURSELF

So much has changed since we wrote this chapter. Differences in gender identity and sexuality are more openly acknowledged, accepted, and discussed. You know your group and we trust that you will be mindful of everyone in the circle. "Love is love." In addition, the myth is a very heterosexual and white Anglo perspective of Aphrodite. As a universal archetype, her skin color varies. Please feel free to adapt the myth with a physical description that represents the girls in your group.

"Do not bring people in your life who weigh you down. And trust your instincts… good relationships feel good. They feel right. They don't hurt. They're not painful. That's not just with somebody you want to marry, but it's with the friends that you choose. It's with the people you surround yourselves with."

~ Michelle Obama

Taking an honest and compassionate look at our own sexual histories, beliefs, and experiences is essential before discussing sexuality with our daughters. Admittedly, this is not necessarily easy, and might require the gentle assistance of a therapist or a wise mentor.

What do you recall about your first sexual experience? What were some of the earliest messages you received from your parents, friends, teachers, and church or religion about sex? What was your overall feeling about sex when you were growing up? How do you feel about your sexuality today? What would you like your daughter to know about her sexuality?

A Note: Lonnie Barbach, author and internationally recognized expert on female sexuality, offers this:

> "Perhaps the most important source of feelings toward sexuality and about a girl's own body comes from messages from her mother. If a mother approaches life positively and freely and then shares her enthusiasm and love, if she holds aspirations for her daughters which move beyond the confines of traditional roles, then it is likely that the child will develop in a less inhibited, more optimistic, self-sufficient, and independent way."

Like the menstruation chapter, there will be all levels of understanding and comfort with this theme. Group members will most likely be curious. For some, sex might feel disgusting, "gross," or even shameful (due to age and immaturity, cultural or religious conditioning, or even unwelcome sexual experiences), while others may over romanticize it. The most important and universal message in this era of #metoo is that they have power over their bodies. Further exploration could include the understanding and importance of consent. These concepts are relevant regardless of gender identity.

CHAPTER THEMES

- Stereotypical sexual behavior depicted in the media
- Sacred sexuality and divine love
- Knowledge is power and empowering our daughters with information
- Virginity and the virgin goddess
- Mother-daughter intimacy

STORIES IN CHAPTER THAT HIGHLIGHT THEMES

Marina's sharing.

CHECK-IN ~ REFLECTIVE QUESTION

The Greek language has seven words for love. We feel different kinds of love for our families, friends, pets, and sometimes even a "crush."

Ask: What is a special love you feel?

READ "The Myth of Aphrodite, Goddess of Love and Beauty"

Ask: What did you hear in the myth? What did you notice as you listened to the story? What stood out for you? What are you curious about? As the facilitator, have some of your own ideas to offer if responses are slow and offer a partial reflection, i.e., "This myth reminds me of..." Or consider the phrase, "I noticed..." then perhaps ask, "What did you notice?" "Noticing" is a power tool!

ART ACTIVITY

LOVE CHARMS

See "Lucky Charms" Chapter 4 in *Moon Mother, Moon Daughter*. These special beads and/or bracelets can represent something different to each girl.

JOURNAL ACTIVITY ~ WRITING AND WITNESSING

Different kinds of love...

Love is...

To love and be loved...

My "Love Charm" bracelet means to me / reminds me...

Facilitator's Notes

This chapter I noticed…

Facilitating this session…

My favorite moment was…

Next time, I will…

Other thoughts:

10
Moon Circle
Weaving the Web of Community

●◑○◐●

The Modern-Day Spider Woman

Today's Spider Woman, the goddess of weaving, is a creator of community. She understands the interconnectedness of all living things and the importance of being inclusive of all. She knows the value of interdependence and creates mutually beneficial relationships in order to both give and receive support. She sees community as a safety net and an expanded source of support for herself and her loved ones. Spider Woman understands the gifts and transcendence that two-spirit members bring to her community. (See "Expanding Our Community" for more.) She knows that asking for help is a sign of strength and confidence, and that helping others nourishes her soul and helps to complete the circle. She lives with a spirit of cooperation.

> "We all have the power to seek communities—friendships, poetry readings, book clubs, even social media groups—where imagination merges with voice to create a fertile soil for new possibilities to merge."
>
> ~ Dr. Tererai Trent, *The Awakened Woman*

◑○◐

PRE-GROUP CONSIDERATION FOR FACILITATORS AND QUESTIONS FOR YOURSELF

Take a look and reflect on the new additional section, "Expanding Our Community" at the end of this chapter, especially if you have a transgender or nonbinary participant in your group. It includes a story with Native American two-spirit identifying rituals, an additional reflective question and prompts. You might also want to consider how you can include this in your Chapter 10 moon circle meeting, as it is an ideal time to discuss the concept of inclusivity and what that means with your participants.

Consider the "The Circle of Friends Myth." It says, "Since the beginning of time, friendship has been the most important relation that woman has experienced. According to the myth, ancient women used to gather around a new fire to celebrate peace and sisterhood among the tribes. The legend tells that if you give a circle of friends to a person you care for, your bonds of friendship will endure forever."

What have been some of your most enduring friendships? How do you experience community? Where do you find support? Who are your strong female role models? What does the term "wise woman" mean to you?

A Note: At this stage preteens and teens are seeking a sense of belonging and are drawn to community and each other, and sometimes it is hard to know "how to be." They often struggle with trying to fit in while being true to their authentic spirit. This is a good opportunity to talk about how to be your unique self in a supportive and loving community. (It's a great reminder for adults, too!)

CHAPTER THEMES

- Friendship and community
- Inclusivity and diversity
- Interconnectedness; sustainability; weaving, the fabric of life
- Heroines, mentors, and role models
- Women's circles

STORIES IN CHAPTER THAT HIGHLIGHT THEMES

Picnic night; Emma's mentor; Millie's friends.

CHECK-IN ~ REFLECTIVE QUESTION

Ask: As you look around the circle, in what ways have we created a community?

READ "The Myth of Spider Woman, Goddess of Weaving"

Ask: What did you hear in the myth? What did you notice as you listened to the story? What stood out for you? What are you curious about? As the facilitator, have some of your own ideas to offer if responses are slow and offer a partial reflection, i.e., "This myth reminds me of…" Or consider the phrase, "I noticed…" then perhaps ask, "What did you notice?" "Noticing" is a power tool!

Younger participants might like to reflect on Charlotte's Web:

> "Far into the night, while the other creatures slept, Charlotte worked on her web. First she ripped out a few of the orb lines near the center. She left the radial lines alone, as they were needed for support. As she worked, her eight legs were a great help to her. So were her teeth. She loved to weave and she was an expert at it."
>
> ~ E. B. White, Charlotte's Web

ART ACTIVITY

WEAVING

Spider woman says: "The most important thing to remember, above all else, is to hold only the most beautiful thoughts in your mind as you weave. You must weave from your heart and your soul."

JOURNAL ACTIVITY ~ WRITING AND WITNESSING

Weaving a web/community…

Being inclusive means…

Our moon circle…

My heroine is…

Making friends…

Like a sister…

WRITE A LETTER TO A FRIEND

You might want to mention some of the small kindnesses she has offered you.

"Friendships between women, as any woman will tell you, are built of a thousand small kindnesses… swapped back and forth and over again."

~ Michelle Obama

Addition to Chapter 10
Expanding Our Community

●◖○◗●

PRE-GROUP CONSIDERATION FOR FACILITATORS AND QUESTIONS FOR YOURSELF

"I'm fully who I am."

~ Elliot Page

Consider the "The Way of the Two-Spirited People." Take some time to familiarize yourself with the two-spirit gender.

How will you ensure a two-spirit, transgender, or nonbinary participant is respectfully included in your group?

A Note: There are three stages of life in which most trans and nonbinary people "come out." One of those is puberty. Participants may be discovering themselves more fully, and identifying in a way that feels more truthful than the gender assigned to them at birth. Make sure participants know your space is not only safe for others who are trans, nonbinary, or two-spirit to join, but is also a safe space for those within the group to share their full selves, even if their understanding of their gender identity is still evolving.

CHECK-IN ~ REFLECTIVE QUESTION

Ask: What does it mean to create safe and respectful space for all participants to be their true selves? What does it mean to be "fully who you are"?

READ "The Way of the Two-Spirited People"

Excerpted and adapted with permission from Sandra Laframboise, "Dancing to Eagle Spirit Society" website.

Native American elders tell of people who were gifted among all beings because they carried two spirits, male and female. These individuals were looked upon as a third and fourth gender and in almost all cultures they were honoured and revered. Two-spirit people were often the visionaries, the healers, the medicine people, mediators, and interpreters of dreams. They were respected as essential members of their ancient cultures and societies.

This two-spirit identity has been documented in over 155 tribes across Native North America. Some tribes had different names for two-spirited men and women. For example, the Din éh (Navaho) refer to them as nàdleehé, or one who is transformed.

Many tribes had rituals for children to go through if they were recognized as acting different from cultural expectations of their assigned birth gender. These rituals ensured the child was truly two-spirit. If parents noticed that a son was disinterested in boyish play or manly work, they would set up a ceremony to determine which way the boy would be brought up. They would make an enclosure of brush, and place in the center both a man's bow and a woman's basket. The boy was told to go inside the circle of brush and to bring something out, and as he entered the brush would be set on fire. The tribe watched what he took with him as he ran out, and if it was the basketry materials they saw him as being two-spirit.

In another ritual, usually carried out when the child is between the ages of nine and twelve, that helped identify a child's two-spirit nature, a singing circle would be prepared, unbeknownst to the boy, involving the whole community as well as distant friends and relatives. On the day of the ceremony everyone gathered around and the boy was led into the middle of the circle. If he remained in the centre, the singer, hidden in the crowd, began to sing the ritual songs and the boy, if he was destined to follow the two-spirit road, started to dance in the fashion of a woman. After the fourth song the boy was declared a two-spirit person and was raised from then on in the appropriate manner, in the Two-Spirit Tradition.

Above all, their childhood was marked by acceptance and understanding by the whole tribe.

Two-Spirit adult people were usually presumed to be people of power. Because they have both maleness and femaleness totally entwined in one body, they were known to be able to 'see' with the eyes of both biological men and biological women. Their extraordinary powers were not questioned.

Ask: What did you hear in the story? What did you notice as you listened to the story? What stood out for you? What are you curious about? As the facilitator, have some of your own ideas to offer if responses are slow and offer a partial reflection, i.e., "This myth reminds me of…" Or consider the phrase, "I noticed…" then perhaps ask, "What did you notice?" "Noticing" is a power tool!

JOURNAL ACTIVITY ~ WRITING AND WITNESSING
(In addition to the ones listed above you could add these prompts.)

Prompts:

Being fully who I am means…

Honoring myself and others…

Facilitator's Notes

This chapter I noticed...

Facilitating this session...

My favorite moment was...

Next time, I will...

Other thoughts:

11
Moon Gift
Giving Back to the World

●◐○◑●

The Modern-Day Kwan Yin

The modern-day Kwan Yin seeks meaning and purpose in her life. She has a compassionate heart and a community spirit. She finds ways to offer meaningful service to her community. She knows that she has unique gifts to discover and share with others. She celebrates her gifts and gives of herself to the world.

◐○◑

"The spirit of service is the heart of humanity."

~ Lailah Gifty Akita, Ghanaian founder of Smart Youth Volunteers Foundation

PRE-GROUP CONSIDERATION FOR FACILITATORS AND QUESTIONS FOR YOURSELF

An authentic gift is a quality possessed on the inside, i.e., compassion, empathy and inspiration.

What authentic gifts do you possess? (Be generous!) How do you see "women's treasures, our collective female gifts?" How do you define "compassion," or experience "compassionate listening"?

It is recommended that you leave some time at the end of this session to plan with the girls for your final meeting and celebration. See Chapter 12, "Moon Dance ~ Celebrating Coming-of-Age" in the original book.

A Note: This is a great age to introduce volunteerism. Encourage participants to volunteer, perhaps at a place where they can explore their interests and natural gifts (e.g., at a local animal shelter, farmer's market, food bank, or senior center). Volunteering is a great "together" activity for a parent and child or friends.

CHAPTER THEMES

- Female gifts
- Giving back / contributing to the world
- Volunteering and community service
- Compassion and compassionate listening

STORIES IN CHAPTER THAT HIGHLIGHT THEMES

Melitta's story; Soul Work and Imaginary Lives; Sidra Stone's dream: female gifts and women's treasures.

CHECK-IN ~ REFLECTIVE QUESTION

Ask: What does it mean to have a special gift? Do you have or know someone who has a special gift? (Facilitators can offer examples.)

READ "The Myth of Kwan Yin—Divine Mother of Compassion"

Ask: What did you hear in the myth? What did you notice as you listened to the story? What stood out for you? What are you curious about? As the facilitator, have some of your own ideas to offer if responses are slow and offer a partial reflection, i.e., "This myth reminds me of..." Or consider the phrase, "I noticed..." then perhaps ask, "What did you notice?" "Noticing" is a power tool!

ART ACTIVITY

GIFT BOX

Create a "gift box" (See section in Chapter 2 of the book, "Prayer Boxes".) You will need small boxes, wrapping paper, scissors, tape, and ribbon; paper and pen to write words to place inside. This gift box can be created to affirm the qualities in oneself (i.e., kind, brave, smart, fun-loving) or to give to another.

JOURNAL ACTIVITY ~ WRITING AND WITNESSING

Prompts:

Like a gift…

My inner/authentic gifts…

Women's treasures…

When I receive a compliment…

When I offer kindness…

This is also fun: "Imaginary Lives" (Read the description on page 133 in the book.) It's inspiring to discover what's already in our imaginations and how close we might be to living these lives.

If I could be…

Or, write from first person present tense and describe your "imaginary life."

I am…

Facilitator's Notes

This chapter I noticed…

Facilitating this session…

My favorite moment was…

Next time, I will…

Other thoughts:

12
Moon Dance
Celebrating Coming-of-Age

●○○○●

The Modern-Day Goddess

The modern-day Goddess honors the sacred in all living things. She values rituals to mark meaningful moments and connect her to the Divine. She knows that coming-of-age is a profound life passage and cause for celebration. As she ventures out into the world, she trusts and is guided by her intuition. She knows that life is an ongoing journey and she is surrounded by a community of wise women who recognize her power.

◐○◑

PRE-GROUP CONSIDERATION FOR FACILITATORS AND QUESTIONS FOR YOURSELF

This chapter is the culmination of your time together and is an opportunity to celebrate with a ritual or ceremony.

What do you remember about your own coming-of-age experience? What marked your rites of passage? What have been your experiences with "rituals"?

A Note: Who doesn't love a party? Usually by this time, the group will have bonded and be ready to have a party. The coming-of-agers will have their own ideas about ways to celebrate. Let them lead the planning (with your wise parameters!). Moms and other adults, with good intentions, may want

"Rituals need to be authentic to you and give you a feeling of connecting with something greater than yourself. My own rituals connect me to the past by keeping me linked to my people and my traditions, and preventing me from losing touch with who I am and where I came from."

~ Dr. Tererai Trent,
The Awakened Woman

to take over and plan—resist this! It's a good exercise for adults to let go and witness the creativity and capabilities of their daughters. And, the planners of the party will feel proud of the ceremony/ritual they have created.

CHAPTER THEMES

- Rituals and celebrations / conscious ritual
- What is a coming-of-age celebration?
- Family and religious traditions
- Unique girls and preferences
- Planning together

STORIES IN CHAPTER THAT HIGHLIGHT THEMES

Janet's birth blessing; a vision quest; Marina's bat mitzvah; Jody's coming-of-age experience; Christyn's and Alisha's coming-of-age celebrations; Mikaila's coming-of-age ceremony.

This chapter will begin in the typical fashion with a reflective question and reading of the myth. Include time for a brief discussion about the "The Women's Society." It's a fascinating retelling of an authentic ritual from a collection of stories passed down by the native people of Vancouver Island and retold by author Anne Cameron. This is one of the stories that inspired us to write *Moon Mother, Moon Daughter*! Most of the rituals included in the book are for modern times.

Plan for the rest of the meeting to be a celebration. We strongly recommend having some sort of ritual or ceremony included in your party. If the group consists solely of coming-of-agers, you may want to consider inviting their significant parent to participate in the ceremony.

CHECK-IN ~ REFLECTIVE QUESTION

Ask: How does it feel to celebrate yourself and each other?

READ "The Myth of The Women's Society"

Ask: What did you hear in the myth? What did you notice as you listened to the story? What stood out for you? What are you curious about? As the facilitator, have some of your own ideas to offer if responses are slow and offer a partial reflection, i.e., "This myth reminds me of…" Or consider the phrase, "I noticed…" then perhaps ask, "What did you notice?" "Noticing" is a power tool!

The Ritual / Ceremony

The following ritual worked well in the groups we facilitated. Of course, you are welcome to adapt this or create your own ritual.

Create an altar together as a grand finale to your shared journey through this book. Instruct each participant to bring two symbols, one representing who they were as a child and the other representing who they are becoming or would like to become. As the facilitator, bring a vase of flowers, one flower per participant. Include candles and any other festive decorations.

Then have the group spend some time journaling an answer to the following statements:

I used to be...

Now I am...

OR:

Looking ahead...

I am becoming...

Simultaneously, have the parents journal a response to this statement:

I have loved watching you become...

Then have each person stand and proclaim their answer and as they do so, present a flower from the vase to their parent. This is a very powerful part of the ceremony. In many ways, it represents how their relationship is changing. In response, the parent will read what they have written and may want to present to their coming-of-ager with a small token/gift (something simple, e.g., a shell, stone, crystal, or jewelry). You may want to discuss the gift choices with participating parents so there is a sense of equal value.

And don't forget a fun feast!

Celebrate your *Moon Mother, Moon Daughter* journey together!!!

Facilitator's Notes and Feedback

Congratulations! Now that you have completed the facilitation of the twelve chapters of *Moon Mother, Moon Daughter* and the final celebratory ceremony, please take some time to reflect on the process and the ways you have grown along with the other participants throughout the journey. You can use any of these prompts for Chapter 12 as well as the overall experience of facilitating the full book of chapters.

This chapter I noticed…

Facilitating the ceremony…

My favorite moment was…

Facilitating moon circles…

I experienced…

My favorite chapter was…

My favorite myth was…

My favorite activity was…

My greatest challenge was…

I learned…

I discovered…

Looking back...

Looking ahead...

I used to be...

Now I am...

Other thoughts:

And now, a note to you:

Thank you so much for using our *Moon Mother, Moon Daughter ~ Moon Circles Facilitator's Guide* to connect and share intimately and authentically with your group and connect them in this spirit with each other. We'd love to hear about your experiences—highlights and challenges—and would love any feedback you'd like to offer us.

Appendix

RESOURCES FOR GENDER DIVERSE INCLUSION

Trans, Nonbinary and General Gender Diverse Inclusive Language

From WebMD.com: "Non-Binary Sex: What It Is"

> "Gender is one of the most complicated human experiences. While many people identify with the gender they were assigned at birth, that's not true for everyone. People who don't identify as their birth gender are called transgender.
>
> Many transgender people identify as men or women, but not all. A significant portion of the population doesn't feel like either gender identity fits them. These people are considered non-binary, because they do not identify as a part of the gender binary of male and female."

References

Dill Werner (dillwerner.com)
Gender, Inc (genderinc.com)
GLADD (glaad.org)
LGBT Equity Center University of Maryland (lgbt.umd.edu)

What Language to Use

Do name it. Say the words: trans/transgender/nonbinary/gender expansive/ gender questioning/cisgender.

Saying the words normalizes the words.

Transgender/trans girl means a person who was assigned male at birth, but is a girl. Transgender/trans boy is a person who was assigned female at birth, but is a boy.

Nonbinary is a person who is neither a boy nor a girl.

Gender fluid is a term some use to describe someone whose gender changes.

Gender questioning is a process of questioning or exploring how a person wants to express their gender identity.

Cisgender/cis is a term for people whose gender identity matches their sex assigned at birth.

PRONOUNS:

DO use the first person pronoun "they"

DO use the gender inclusive terms: child, parent/caregiver/partner

DO use the phrase "women/girls and people of marginalized genders"

What language NOT to use:

Instead of "___ identifies as nonbinary," DO use "___ is nonbinary."

Instead of "___ are her preferred pronouns," DO use "___ are her pronouns."

Instead of "___ was born a man" or "biologically male," DO use "___ was assigned male at birth."

Assumptions and Normalcy

Normalize different experiences of being a girl coming-of-age. For example, not all women bleed and not all people who bleed are women.

Not every woman has a vulva and not every man has a penis. Phrases such as "when a woman gets her period… " are not as inclusive as "when a person with a uterus gets their period…"

Coming-of-Age as a Trans/Nonbinary/Two-Spirit/Gender Nonconforming Person

BOOKS AND ARTICLES BY "OWN VOICES" AUTHORS

Dale, Laura Kate. *Uncomfortable Labels* (memoir by a nonbinary, gay, autistic person)

Kobabe, Maia. *Gender Queer: A Memoir* (graphic novel memoir)

Minus18.org. *"I JUST CAME OUT AS NON-BINARY, HERE'S WHAT THAT MEANS"*

Tobia, Jacob. *Sissy: A Coming of Gender Story* (a nonbinary person's life story)

Windlust, Jamie. *In Their Shoes* (memoir by a nonbinary person)

Whitney, Emerson. *Heaven* (a nonbinary person's coming-of-age story, which specifically traces the evolution of their gender through their relationship with their mother)

Wong, Alice, *Editor. Disability Visibility* (specifically about disability via an intersectional lens) with essays by:

Jen Deerinwater (two-spirit, bisexual, disabled journalist)

Leah Lakshmi Piepzna-Samarasinha (queer, disabled, nonbinary writer)

Liz Moore (chronically ill, neurodivergent, nonbinary writer)

Mari Ransawakh (disabled, nonbinary writer)

Sky Cubacub (nonbinary, queer, disabled, Filipinx artist)

OTHER "OWN VOICES"

Alok Vaid-Menon (gender nonconforming poet, artist, and advocate who uses Instagram to share their story)

Travis Alabanza (Black, nonbinary artist/writer)

Amrou Al-Kadhi (nonbinary Muslim writer/performer)

Sherent Mishitashin Harris (young two-spirit activist)

Mythology and Story in the Gender Expansive Community

TWO-SPIRITED PEOPLE

Dancing to Eagle Spirit Society (dancingtoeaglespiritsociety.org)

NATIVE AMERICAN COMMUNITIES

Over 150 Native American tribes have documented and honored two-spirit people. These are some specific cultures and myths:

Nadleehi in Navajo culture (likely to bring wealth to their household, appreciated as mediator)

Turquoise Boy and White Shell Girl in Navajo Mythology

Kwasaitaka people in the Hopi culture

Kyanakwe people in the Zuni culture

MORE CULTURES AND MYTHS

Lan Caihe in Chinese Mythology

Kinnar or Hijra people in India

Lakapati God in Filipinx mythology

Note: The above cultures have a history of recognizing genders beyond the binary and in some cases also have mythology surrounding them. In the west, ruling religions have not allowed trans/nonbinary/gender nonconforming people to live as themselves, let alone have a mythological celebration of their coming-of-age. And though our country has a history of silencing and murdering trans nonbinary/gender nonconforming people, they have existed as long as any of us, with a history to match.

Additional Resources

Bolen, Jean Shinoda. *The Millionth Circle ~ How to Change Ourselves and the World*. Conari Press, 1999.

Corinna, Heather, Isabella Rotman and Luke Howard. *Wait, What?: A Comic Book Guide to Relationships, Bodies, and Growing Up.* Limerence Press, 2019.

Silverberg, Cory. *You Know, Sex ~ Bodies, Gender, Puberty, and Other Things.* Triangle Square, 2022.

Simon, Rachel E. *The Every Body Book ~ The LGBTQ+ Inclusive Guide for Kids about Sex, Gender, Bodies, and Families.* Jessica Kingsley Publishers, 2020.

Taylor, Sonya Renee. *The Body is Not an Apology ~ The Power of Radical Self Love.* Rockridge Press, 2018.

Taylor, Sonya Renee. *Celebrate Your Body ~ The Ultimate Puberty Book for Girls.* Second Edition. Berrett-Koehler Publishers, 2021.

Trent, Tererai, Ph.D. *The Awakened Woman ~ A Guide for Remembering & Igniting Your Sacred Dreams.* Atria/Enliven Books, 2018.

Weschler, Toni. *Cycle Savvy ~ The Smart Teen's Guide to the Mysteries of Her Body.* William Morrow Paperbacks, 2006.

Gratitudes and Acknowledgments

Since the first publication in 2002, M*oon Mother, Moon Daughter ~ Myths and Rituals that Celebrate a Girl's Coming-of-Age* has been circling the globe, finding her way to women everywhere. We are eternally grateful to all the women who were inspired to use our book with their daughters, in their communities, and create their own mother-daughter moon circles. We've been inspired by you! Over the years, you've reached out, affirmed the value of our book, and asked for more.

In response, we endeavored to create this companion, *Moon Mother, Moon Daughter ~ Moon Circles Facilitator's Guide*. Along the way, we discovered we had an opportunity to create a more inclusive version of the original book, to reflect and represent a more expansive expression of the feminine (as we're certain our universal Moon Goddess intended!).

We are grateful to Erika Römer, Executive Director at Seven Seas Press, for her vision, clarity, and guidance throughout this project and the many concrete contributions she made; also, to Creative Director, Colleen McCarthy-Evans, who offered her creative eye to the overall design.

We were blessed to be joined and supported by others throughout the process, who offered their gifts and generous contributions:

Caitlyn McDermott, mama of Emmie and Ida, for the "Resources for Gender Diverse Inclusion; Trans, Nonbinary and General Gender Diverse Inclusive Language; Coming-of-Age as a Trans/Nonbinary/Two-Spirit/ Gender nonconforming person" found in the Appendix; she helped to ensure our language throughout the Guide was respectful and inclusive. Cait's early reflection sparked our hearts and fueled our commitment to making this guide inclusive of all when she shared:

"While looking into all this, I couldn't help but think about what the lack of material really reflected. That kids like mine have not been allowed to come of age, not as themselves at least. That their stories haven't been written, because they have had to hide them to stay alive. That they have never been celebrated, only shamed. I know the world is changing for the better, I can feel it, and I am so grateful it is. But I can't help think of all the trans and nonbinary stories we will never know. What light they could have given my kid, what beauty they could have given us all."

We were fortunate to find "Dancing to Eagle Spirit Society," the website of Sandra Laframboise and Michael Anhorn, and are grateful for their generous permission to use an excerpt from "THE WAY OF THE TWO SPIRITED PEOPLE."

Nancy Whittaker, for lending her heart and eagle eye to the initial proofing of the manuscript and making subtle and significant changes.

Michelle Levy, copy editor extraordinaire, whose passion for this project infused it with experience, wisdom and love. What an unexpected gift!

Isaac Hernández de Lipa, who helped with the design adaptation for the Second Edition and brought his creative genius to this journey.

It's been a delight to reconnect with Helen D'Souza, the artist of the original book cover and cover of this *Facilitator's Guide,* who created a new cover for our *By the Light of the Moon ~ A Moon Mother, Moon Daughter Companion Journal.* We trust you'll find this to be another exquisite work of art, and an additional resource for your moon circles.

And once again, to all the girls whose original stories we shared, who have become bright full moon goddesses, many of them now mamas.

About the Authors

Janet Lucy, MA, is the co-author of *Moon Mother, Moon Daughter ~ Myths and Rituals that Celebrate a Girl's Coming-of-Age*, award-winning author of *Makana is a Gift / Makana es un Regalo, Mermaid Dreams / Sueños de Sirena*, and *The Three Sunflowers / Los Tres Girasoles*. She is the Founder / Director of Women's Creative Network (WCN) in Santa Barbara, CA, where she offers consulting for intuitive, creative and professional development; facilitates women's weekly writing circles, workshops and trainings, and international retreats. Janet teaches and guides "Divine Ink ~ Illuminating the Heroine's Journey," a divine feminine path to transformation. Janet loves to share her divine inspiration with other women. www.janetlucyink.com

Terri Allison is the co-author of *Moon Mother, Moon Daughter ~ Myths and Rituals that Celebrate a Girl's Coming-of-Age*. She has been a teacher and educational administrator for over 40 years, in programs for infants through adults. She has completed a fellowship in Parent-Infant Mental Health from the University of Boston, Mass. and has a Post Graduate Certificate from the Napa Fellowship Program's Reflective Supervision, Consultation and Facilitation Academy. Terri currently runs her own consulting company, Moonlit Consulting, with a primary focus on Early Childhood Education and Reflective Practice. She offers private sessions, small group learning communities and trainings for educators, parents and leaders in the field of early care and education.

About Seven Seas Press

Seven Seas Press collaborates with authors, artists and translators to create content with sensitivity and depth, that honors and reflects our diverse humanity. Through our nonprofit we create partnerships with local and international organizations, who share our vision to empower, nurture and contribute to the lives of others. Seven Seas Press is a 501(c)3 Public Charity EIN 83-0792556. Please visit us at: sevenseaspress.org

Please follow us on Facebook at Moon Mother, Moon Daughter and Instagram @moonmothermoondaughter

Books by the Authors and Seven Seas Press

Moon Mother, Moon Daughter ~ Myths and Rituals that Celebrate a Girl's Coming-of-Age co-authored by Janet Lucy and Terri Allison

The Three Sunflowers by Janet Lucy, illustrated by Colleen McCarthy-Evans

Mermaid Dreams by Janet Lucy, illustrated by Colleen McCarthy-Evans

Makana is a Gift by Janet Lucy, illustrated by Alexis Cantu

The Little Blue Dragon written and illustrated by Colleen McCarthy-Evans

Why Am I by Colleen McCarthy-Evans, illustrated by Sarah Dietz

The Crazy Old Maid by Colleen McCarthy-Evans, illustrated by Janneke Ipenburg

Versiones bilingües / Bilingual versions:

The Three Sunflowers / Los Tres Girasoles (English / Spanish)

Три Соняшники / The Three Sunflowers (Ukrainian / English)

Sueños de Sirena / Mermaid Dreams

Makana es un Regalo / Makana is a Gift

The Little Blue Dragon / La Dragoncita Azul

Por Qué Soy / Why Am I

La Vieja Criada Loca / The Crazy Old Maid

Made in the USA
Las Vegas, NV
13 August 2023

76048177R00063